PRAISE

"Beth Felker Jones provides a series of devotions during the specific seasons of the COVID-19 pandemic that speak into that pandemic, but yet these devotions will continue to speak to us—as acts of memory, as acts of pondering, as acts of lament, as acts of trust, and as acts of hope. Quarantine, she tells us, can't stop Easter. *Pandemic Prayers* comes from a Christian, a mother, a professor, and an author. As a theologian Beth Felker Jones takes us to spiritual giants like Julian of Norwich, and as a devotional Christian she expresses her annoyance and her pain with the pandemic, but she opens her heart for all to see who she is, like the Bible's own prayers and devotions."

—SCOT MCKNIGHT, AUTHOR OF *OPEN TO THE SPIRIT* AND *THE JESUS CREED*

"In this short book, Beth Felker Jones has given us a rich and beautiful gift. Her writing is vivid, comforting, and luminescent. And she masterfully pulls together her daily life and struggles amid a global pandemic and enduring truths from the great tradition of Christian thought. With wide-ranging meditations on anxiety, lament, weakness, death, and hope, Jones invites us into the mystery of God with the clarity of a brilliant theologian and the compassionate heart of a pastor."

—TISH HARRISON WARREN, AUTHOR OF *LITURGY OF THE ORDINARY: SACRED PRACTICES IN EVERYDAY LIFE*

"In times of stress, Christians are often driven to seek a deeper prayer life. This book is both the fruit of such a search as well as a guide to one. It is unhurriedly calming and quietly fortifying. In the shadow of illness, social unrest, and an uncertain global future, I plan to keep it on my nightstand and return to it often for nourishment and comfort."

—WESLEY HILL, AUTHOR OF *SPIRITUAL FRIENDSHIP*

"We live in a strange world where things like pandemics and global warming seem to be the new norm. If truth be told, many of us don't know how to pray in times of crisis. In *Pandemic Prayers*, theologian Beth Felker Jones teaches us how to pray in difficult seasons of life by sharing her own very personal reflections in the form of devotions and rich theological prayers. This book has blessed my life and I pray that it may help you find fresh faith, hope, and healing in these uncertain times."

—Winfield Bevins, author of *Ever Ancient Ever New*

"In *Pandemic Prayers*, Beth Felker Jones offers reflections and prayers to accompany us in the dark valley of Coronavirus. Avoiding simplistic platitudes, she faces the pain of this current moment head-on. And, with deep wisdom and vulnerability, brings the reader face to face with Jesus."

—Emily H. McGowin, author of *Quivering Families*

"What a gift to have these devotions written by a wise theologian with a compassionate spirit and gift for words. Though written during a pandemic, they will inspire us to find hope in God whatever season of life we are in, since life is never as stable and predictable as we would like it to be. These devotions touched my heart, gave me courage, and led me to prayer."

—L. Roger Owens, author of *Threshold of Discovery: A Field Guide to Spirituality in Midlife*

*To Jamie, with great love on your 2021 Birthday. I hope this book will bring you hope for better days & months ahead as it does for me.
Love, your best M.L.,
S*

Pandemic Prayers

Pandemic Prayers

Devotions and Prayers for a Crisis

BETH FELKER JONES

Afterword by Andrew D. Kinsey

CASCADE *Books* • Eugene, Oregon

PANDEMIC PRAYERS
Devotions and Prayers for a Crisis

Copyright © 2021 Beth Felker Jones. All rights reserved. Except for brief quotations in critical publications or reviews, no part of this book may be reproduced in any manner without prior written permission from the publisher. Write: Permissions, Wipf and Stock Publishers, 199 W. 8th Ave., Suite 3, Eugene, OR 97401.

New Revised Standard Version Bible, copyright © 1989 the Division of Christian Education of the National Council of the Churches of Christ in the United States of America. Used by permission. All rights reserved.

Cascade Books
An Imprint of Wipf and Stock Publishers
199 W. 8th Ave., Suite 3
Eugene, OR 97401

www.wipfandstock.com

PAPERBACK ISBN: 978-1-7252-7954-4
HARDCOVER ISBN: 978-1-7252-7955-1
EBOOK ISBN: 978-1-7252-7956-8

Cataloguing-in-Publication data:

Names: Jones, Beth Felker, 1976–, author. | Kinsey, Andrew, afterword.

Title: Pandemic prayers : devotions and prayers for a crisis / Beth Felker Jones ; afterword by Andrew D. Kinsey.

Description: Eugene, OR : Cascade Books, 2021.

Identifiers: ISBN 978-1-7252-7954-4 (paperback) | ISBN 978-1-7252-7955-1 (hardcover) | ISBN 978-1-7252-7956-8 (ebook)

Subjects: LCSH: Prayers.

Classification: BV245 .J65 2021 (paperback) | BV245 .J65 (ebook)

02/05/21

Contents

About this Book   ix

PART I | BEGINNINGS

God's Unchanging Faithfulness	3
Grief and What Is Good	6
Martin Luther against the Terrors	9
I Have Called You My Friends	13

PART II | PRAYING WITH JULIAN

Windows for Prayer	19
The Blood of Jesus for a World in Need	23
The Kind God Makes Us Kin	27
God's Response to Sin Is Jesus	31
Hope Instead of Cheer	35

PART III | PSALMS OF LAMENT

God Hears Our Cries	41
On Not Being Okay	44
Lament for Injustice	46

Telling the Truth   48
Love and Lament   50

PART IV | THE WAY OF THE CROSS

Pour It Out (Written for the Beginning of Holy Week 2020)   55
Jesus Shares Our Grief   59
God with Us   61
Love to the End (From Maundy Thursday)   64
Jesus against the Enemy (From Good Friday)   68

PART V | RESURRECTION

Weird Easter   73
Easter between the Times   76
Labor Pains   79
Continuity and Transformation   83
In My Side   87
Keeping On   90

Afterword by Andrew D. Kinsey   93
About the Author   95

About this Book

THE LITTLE BOOK YOU'RE holding was written during the first weeks of the COVID-19 pandemic in the United States. As the reality of the situation began to settle over us, I wondered how I might best love my neighbor in such a time. Since I'm a writer, I decided I would write.

Besides being a writer, I'm a theology teacher, and I believe with all my being that the great truths of the faith will give strength to us as we live as disciples of Jesus Christ. I've tried, here, to connect some of those truths to our ordinary existence in a time of fear and suffering. I've tried to show how the truth about God revealed in Scripture (which is what theology is) matters here and now.

These devotions are offered as an act of love towards you, the reader, but they were and are also a coping mechanism for me. The words here were written as much to myself as to any other audience, as I, like all of us, need constant reminders to turn to God in prayer.

I wrote these words quarantined at home with my family, and I offer these reflections and prayers in the hope that they might point us to the love of God as we continue to go through the pandemic crisis together and as we finally emerge from that crisis.

The devotions printed here were written during March and April of 2020, during the first weeks my state of Illinois was on

ABOUT THIS BOOK

order to stay at home in an effort to slow the spread of the novel coronavirus. As you read them, you'll see how they come out of those weeks, as I struggled with the day to day of what was weighing on us all.

But pain, uncertainty, and suffering are always realities we face in this life, and I hope these devotions will speak to other days than those on which they were written.

PART I

Beginnings

God's Unchanging Faithfulness

Today, people in my state are on lockdown at home, a lockdown ordered by our governor.

As fear and uncertainty about the coronavirus spreads, it's hard for me to believe that, just a week ago, I was in Mexico with a friend. (Feel free to let me know I shouldn't have gone to Mexico. Hindsight, and all that).

My friend and I were feeling the weight of work and wanted to escape the grey Illinois skies for a little bit of sunshine therapy. Each day, as we sat at the beach, we checked our phones and reeled at the news as our world changed in shocking ways.

We both teach at Wheaton College, a place that has taken only two snow days in the decade-plus that I've worked there, and we could not have imagined the college's decision to close for the semester.

Now we were in Mexico, far from the work we care about and the people we love, trying to love our people through e-mail and social media. In our few days away, everything changed. For us and for everyone we knew.

Many of us—certainly me—hate change. We like our steady routine, our predictable pattern.

Every teaching semester, I watch students settle into the same seats for every class session, returning to the front row, or the middle left, or the way back. Every Sunday, I herd my children into the same pew and settle in as other church folk take their usual places.

Now, nobody can take their normal seat or their usual pew.

The temptation here is to scold, to say, "Change is inevitable. Suck it up. Grow up."

I don't think that's what we should be saying.

I think we can recognize something true and good in our aversion to change.

We human beings are so very vulnerable (though we like to pretend that we aren't), and stability helps us to live through our vulnerability.

But the stability we need isn't really in a usual seat. The stability we need is in God.

We can count on God. In the midst of our suffering change, God is the one who-is-who-he-is-and-will-be-who-he-will-be.

Christian theologians through the centuries have taught that God is immutable. God does not mutate.

God does not change.

Early church fathers liked to quote Malachi 3:6 here: "For I the Lord do not change." James speaks of the Father as the one "with whom there is no variation or shadow due to change" (1:17).

This teaching has gone out of style in contemporary theology, as some complain that it makes God into a cold, unfeeling monolith. But the best of Christian teaching has never understood it so. God's immutability does not make him into some philosophical caricature.

God's immutability is God's steadfast love.

When Malachi proclaims that the Lord does not change, he tells us that *this* is the reason God's people are able to persist: "I the Lord do not change; therefore you, O children of Jacob, have not perished."

The children of Jacob live, because of God's steadfast love.

When James invokes the "no variation" nature of God, he does it in the context of the good gifts that come to us from the Father. That unchanging Father is the one who sends "every perfect gift" (Jas 1:17).

Or, in the words of the hymn by Thomas Chisholm, who was riffing on James:

> Great is Thy faithfulness, O God my Father;
> There is no shadow of turning with Thee,
> Thou changest not, Thy compassions they fail not,
> As Thou hast been, Thou forever wilt be.

Our world is being rocked. We're uncertain about the future.

And it's okay to admit that this is hard.

Through the difficulty of change, we can lean on the God whose compassions will never fail.

We can't sit in our familiar seats, at school, or church, or work. But God remains familiar. God remains unchanging compassion.

God is still and always will be steadfast love.

All I can do today is pray that God would help me to lean into that truth.

Holy God,

Thank you for your unchanging faithfulness. Thank you for your unfailing compassion. Thank you for being the one who keeps your promises. Help us to know that you are here with us as we suffer change and uncertainty, and remind us of Jesus, who suffered with us so that we might know your steadfast love.

In the name of the Father, the Son, and the Holy Spirit,

Amen.

Grief and What Is Good

Today, my husband is in Indiana with our oldest child.

They're packing up her dorm room and driving her home. This is her first year of college, and she's been thriving like crazy—just eating it up: the friends, the freedom, the community.

It's such a loss for her to have to come home.

My heart breaks for the seniors in high school and college who are losing their last days with friends, their last proms, senior banquets, and nights spent talking and laughing together.

It's a huge loss.

I can see the faces of our seniors at the college where I teach, and I'm holding them before God in my heart.

There are so many losses right now.

Vacations. Celebrations. Planned evenings with friends.

And there are going to be many more, and we know they are going to be harder.

Jobs. Mental health. Precious human beings.

As we go through this crisis, hear this:

It's okay to feel the losses.

It's okay to ache as carefully laid plans have to be put away.

It's okay to grieve.

One of the most fundamental truths of Christian faith is this: creation is good.

God made the world, God loves the world, and God has good purposes for the world. Just read the first chapter of Genesis and notice how many times the word "good" is used.

All those things we care about? They matter. God cares about them too.

The early church rejected the false teaching known as Gnosticism. Gnosticism taught that spiritual reality is good, while material reality is evil.

Against this, the church leaned on what Scripture shows us about God as creator. Creation is not evil. God made it, God loves it, and God has good purposes for it.

Paul is talking about a Gnostic-like teaching when he writes against those who "forbid marriage and demand abstinence from foods" (1 Tim 4:3). We know this instinct: the instinct to look at the delights of this world and turn up one's nose, to try to be above the joys of feasts and warm human love.

I've seen a lot of rhetoric in this pandemic that would spiritualize our faith and minimize the real human losses we're going through. This rhetoric says, "Your silly celebrations don't matter. Only spiritual things matter."

But God's revelation here teaches us otherwise. God created feasts and flesh "to be received with thanksgiving . . . for everything created by God is good, and nothing is to be rejected, provided it is received with thanksgiving" (1 Tim 4:3-4).

God made these joys, God loves these joys, and we receive these joys with thanksgiving.

The joys of this life are precious. Friends laughing together in a dorm are precious. Youth groups playing silly games together are precious. The chance to be together is precious.

And when we lose these things, it's okay to say "ouch."

Our God is the God who made this world and loves it.

Our God is the God who cares about the intimate realities of our lives.

And our God is the God who knows our grief. He's carried it in his very flesh, in the body of Jesus.

While my husband packs the dorm room, I'm making room for our daughter to come home.

I'm rearranging, stacking up outgrown books to donate, making space for her stuff, dusting off shelves and her piano, and taking down pictures so she can hang what she wants.

I wish I could give her something that would make up for her losses. I can't.

But I'm doing what I can. The space I'm cleaning for her is not what I want it to be, but I'm making room anyway, hoping to give her a soft place to land, and to grieve the losses, and to welcome the unexpected gains that will come as we go through this together.

We can treat our losses with tenderness, as God our Father treats us tenderly.

Gracious God,

Thank you for being the one who made and loves the world. Be with us as we grieve the many precious things we're having to let go of right now. Let us know that you have room for our losses, that our lives and losses matter to you, and help us to turn to you for solace and comfort. Remind of us Jesus, who took our pain into his flesh, so that we might know your love.

In the name of the Father, the Son, and the Holy Spirit, Amen.

Martin Luther against the Terrors

LAST SEMESTER, I TAUGHT a class on what Christians believe about the Holy Spirit and the last things (pneumatology and eschatology, in theology-speak).

One of the readings I assigned was the Protestant Reformer Martin Luther's pastoral letter from the year 1527, "Whether One May Flee from a Deadly Plague."[1]

We read the piece as a bit of "practical theology," connecting Christian belief to Christian life. (Yes, I really do believe that eschatology and pneumatology matter for our daily lives; I'm a teacher, after all.)

Enough with the "-ologies" though, what did Luther have to say about plagues?

In the midst of one of the most terrible plagues imaginable, he writes a pastoral letter about neighbor love.

He reminds his readers of our obligations to one another.

Pastors need to take care of their people. Those in public office need to take care of their cities. Parents need to care for their children.

And he reminds us that we're not alone in this:

---

1. The whole text is available online or in Lull and Russell's collection *Martin Luther's Basic Theological Writings*, 3rd ed. (Minneapolis: Fortress, 2012).

PART I | BEGINNINGS

"We are bound to each other in such a way that no one may forsake the other in his distress."

And then Luther navigates a distinctively Christian way of dealing with the threat of death. Life is good, and it is to be protected. At the same time, death has been overcome in Jesus, and so it has no ultimate say over us.

When neighbor love, including self-love, means keeping safe, we keep safe, and when it means risking death, we risk it freely because we know that, in Christ, we have everlasting life.

Luther's confidence is in God. He reminds us to cling to God's promises and to what Christ has done for us.

Neighbor love can mean risking everything, even death, by being physically present for others. I'm praying today for those who are doing just that. Health care workers. Cleaning crews. Caregivers. Cashiers. Cooks. Warehouse workers. Delivery drivers. Pharmacists. Sanitation workers. Custodians. Government workers. People sweating it out to restock the grocery store shelves. And so many others.

Luther would have us "take courage in the fact that we are mutually bound together."

After building people up for risky neighbor love, Luther also has words for people who don't take the plague seriously:

> They are rash and reckless, tempting God and disregarding everything that might counteract death and the plague. They disdain the use of medicines, they do not avoid places and persons infected by the plague, but lightheartedly make sport of it and wish to prove how independent they are. . . . This is not trusting God but tempting him. . . . Such people behave as though a house were burning in the city and nobody were trying to put the fire out. Instead they give leeway to the flames so that the whole city is consumed. . . . If some are so foolish as

to not take precautions but aggravate the contagion, then the devil has a field day and many will die.[2]

Neighbor love can mean staying home. It can mean self-isolating to prevent the spread of disease and to protect others, especially those who are most vulnerable.

Quarantine is what neighbor love looks like for most of us, here at the beginning of this pandemic. And that kind of neighbor love is also risky, painful, and self-sacrificial. (I can't tell you how many texts I've exchanged in the last few days, just trying to keep it together while staying home.)

I'm praying today for those who are doing hard things to love their neighbors this way. Students. Teachers. Parents. Those who are alone and lonely. And so many others.

With Luther, we can speak back to the devil, who would terrorize us out of loving our neighbor as God would have us do:

> Get away, you devil, with your terrors! . . . If you can terrorize, Christ can strengthen me. If you can kill, Christ can give life. If you have poison in your fangs, Christ has far greater medicine. Should not my dear Christ, with his precepts, his kindness, and all his encouragement, be more important in my spirit than you, roguish devil, with your false terrors in my weak flesh? God forbid. Get away devil! Here is Christ, and here am I, his servant in his work. Let Christ prevail.[3]

Today, Luther is inspiring me to try to speak back against all evil, to claim Christ's strength and power to love my neighbors in this time.

Loving God,

Thank you for being the one who loves us and empowers us to love our neighbors. Be with all who are doing hard things for

---

2. *Martin Luther's Basic Theological Writings*, 748.
3. *Martin Luther's Basic Theological Writings*, 745.

neighbor love today. Give us strength against the terrors that haunt us, and remind us of Jesus, who showed us how to love our neighbors in his life and made it possible for us to rightly love you and one another, through his work on the cross and in his resurrection.

In the name of the Father, the Son, and the Holy Spirit,

Amen.

I Have Called You My Friends

TODAY, WE COME TO the end of the first work week in which many of us in the United States have started working remotely, or supervising children who are schooling remotely, or going to work in deeply changed circumstances.

And I'm thinking a lot about how grateful I am for friends.

I'm grateful for the people whom I usually see at work, who are now sending social media updates to help each other transition to online teaching. I'm grateful for old friends who have touched base to check in during this crazy time. I'm grateful for quick texts to vent or encourage or empathize. I'm grateful that my youngest son got to connect online with his school friends for a reading lesson, and that I got to see him literally jumping with joy at seeing the faces of his friends.

And I'm missing my friends.

I'd trade a lot for some in-person lunch with friends right now, complete with chicken fingers, long conversation, and lots of laughs.

I'm grateful for one of the most extraordinary things Jesus ever said:

"I have called you my friends" (John 15:15).

Jesus is the Lord of all, the Alpha and the Omega, Son of God and Son of Man, the light of the world, the King of the universe.

And Jesus is our friend.

PART I | BEGINNINGS

If we can even begin to glimpse the truth of this, we will be overwhelmed by the love of God.

Here, the holy, transcendent, eternal God makes himself intimate to us. God doesn't stand far off; God wants to be in real relationship with us. Jesus is here for us. He enters into the most ordinary and difficult realities of our daily lives. Any frustration or joy that we might want to share with a friend is something we can share with Jesus, and his Father, and his Spirit.

Jesus is truly our friend.

Joseph Scriven's nineteenth-century hymn is speaking to me today:

> What a friend we have in Jesus,
> All our sins and griefs to bear!
> What a privilege to carry
> Everything to God in prayer!

In this crisis, love from friends has been more precious than ever. Absence of friends has been more painful than ever.

In this crisis, the friendship of Jesus is as real as ever, but we may be more aware of our need for it than we ever have been.

As friends of Jesus, we're called to "love one another" (John 15:12) as he has loved us.

We're reminded that "no one has greater love than this, to lay down one's life for one's friends" (John 15:13). Jesus laid down his life for us, and as his friends, we can find the courage to pour out our lives for each other, to face the challenges of each new day.

And when human friends are not there for us, Jesus is.

> Do thy friends despise, forsake thee?
> Take it to the Lord in prayer!
> In His arms He'll take and shield thee,
> Thou wilt find a solace there.

It's the end of a whirlwind week, and I'm drained. I'm praying to remember to turn to my friend Jesus to seek that solace which only his friendship can provide.

Heavenly Father,

Thank you for sending us your Son, Jesus Christ, so that we might know that you are with us and for us. Thank you for allowing us to bring all the intimacies of our sorrows to you. Remind us of Jesus, whose friendship is a sure and steady reality today and every day.

In the name of the Father, the Son, and the Holy Spirit,

Amen.

PART II

Praying with Julian

Windows for Prayer

THE VIEW OUT MY window this morning is all fluffy snow and empty street. It's peaceful and beautiful . . .
    And I'm not the only one going stir crazy anyway.
    My heart is unquiet. My temptations are to self-absorption. This suggests, to me, that it's time to pray.
    "Rejoice in hope, be patient in suffering, persevere in prayer" (Rom 12:2).

My friend Julian of Norwich did her praying in the fourteenth and early fifteenth centuries. I call her my friend because she's been there for me in lots of trying times. Maybe you'll find that she's there for you too.
    Her book, *Revelations of Divine Love*,[1] is the first book of theology written by a woman in the English language. We don't know her real name, but we call her Julian because it was the name of her church.
    Julian lived two lives.
    The first was a life in the world: a life of household concerns and running into neighbors on the street. We don't know for certain, but it's likely she was married and had children.

---

    1. All of my quotations come from *The Complete Julian of Norwich* (Paraclete Giants Series), ed. Fr. John Julian (Brewster, MA: Paraclete, 2009).

PART II | PRAYING WITH JULIAN

The bubonic plague ravished her town twice during her lifetime. About a quarter of the population would have died. We don't know for sure, but it's likely she lost her family to the plague.

Then, Julian's life in the world ended (as we may feel ours is ending, or at least is on a painful and indefinite pause).

Julian's second life was lived as an anchoress. She was walled away from the world.

Bear with me, because this is going to sound incredibly strange if you haven't heard of it before. The life of an anchoress was a dedicated ministry to a church and a town. The anchoress (or anchorite, if a man) was walled into a cell, or anchor-hold, attached to a church.

Julian would have stepped into her cell, and then stone walls went up. She wouldn't leave until her death.

But this wasn't a burial alive or a denial of the world God loves. Even though it was a life set apart, it was still a life for the world.

In her little room, her anchor-hold, Julian would have had three windows:

One to the street.

One to the sanctuary.

One to care for her needs. (Food. Laundry. Books. Presumably, the chamber pot.)

Even though it was a life set apart, it was still a life for the world.

Julian was there to pray in place. To stay put in order to commit herself, body and soul, to prayer for those outside those windows.

In fourteenth-century Norwich, you couldn't call your pastor or text a friend, but if you needed prayer, day or night, you knew where Julian would be, and you could talk to her through her window.

Imagine Julian. Perhaps she's walking back and forth in her 9′ x 11′ anchor-hold. Perhaps she's sewing. Perhaps she's looking through her window towards the altar in the church.

WINDOWS FOR PRAYER

She's praying.

But is she feeling the warm presence of God? Is her face aglow with peace? Is she able to pray without her attention wandering?

Maybe. But maybe not.

Julian says that when we pray, "frequently our trust is not complete, for we are not certain that God hears us . . . because we feel absolutely nothing (for we are frequently as barren and dry after our prayers as we were before)."[2]

Reflecting on such emptiness in prayer, Julian tells us that the Lord showed her something wonderful:

"I am the ground of thy praying."[3]

Prayer isn't about us. It's about God. In this, says Julian, "our good Lord shows a powerful encouragement."

"It is not our praying that is the cause of the goodness and grace that He does for us, but God's own characteristic goodness."

"I am the ground of thy praying."

That's what God showed to Julian.

And she counsels us, "Our good Lord wills that this be recognized by His lovers on earth, and the more that we recognize this, the more we shall pray."

"Pray in the Spirit at all times in every prayer and supplication. To that end keep alert and always persevere in supplication for all the saints" (Eph 6:18).

Julian encourages us to "pray inwardly, even though it seems to give thee no pleasure."

Pray, "though thou sensest nothing."

Pray, "though thou seest nothing."

Pray, "though thou thinkest thou canst achieve nothing."[4]

Julian wants us to find freedom and trust in knowing that God is the "ground of thy praying."

2. Julian, *Revelations of Divine Love*, 41.
3. Julian, *Revelations of Divine Love*, 41.
4. Julian, *Revelations of Divine Love*, 41.

> Do not worry about anything, but in everything by prayer and supplication with thanksgiving let your requests be made known to God. And the peace of God, which surpasses all understanding, will guard your hearts and your minds in Christ Jesus. (Phil 4:6–7)

In quarantine, we're like Julian. We still have windows. I'm praying today that God would help me to turn to my windows to pray for and love the world.

Maybe this time and space of being walled in can become an anchor-hold.

Maybe we can find a new freedom for prayer.

Maybe Julian's experience can set us free from our own desperate efforts to get our prayers right. In the truth that prayer is about what God does and not about what we are doing, Julian finds comfort from "all our doubtful fears."[5]

> I call upon you, for you will answer me, O God;
>   incline your ear to me, hear my words.
> Wondrously show your steadfast love,
>   O savior of those who seek refuge
>   from their adversaries at your right hand. (Ps 17:6–7)

Loving Father,

Help us to lean on you in prayer. Help us to make our lives an anchor-hold. Help us to love the world through the windows you provide. And, please God, remind us of Jesus, whose work allows us to pray in confidence and trust, because he's made us your sons and daughters.

In the name of the Father, the Son, and the Holy Spirit,

Amen.

---

5. Julian, *Revelations of Divine Love*, 42.

The Blood of Jesus for a World in Need

YESTERDAY, I WROTE ABOUT the medieval Christian writer Julian of Norwich and her life of prayer in an anchor-hold. Today, I'm thinking more about what was going on in Julian's world and the ways she might help us as we face this pandemic.

Julian's world was crumbling.

Two times during Julian's life, the plague swept through the English town of Norwich. The pandemic took a third of Europe's population.

It was terrifying in its contagiousness and efficiency, and because people didn't know how it was transmitted, fear and misguided attempts at self-protection were rampant.

There were too many bodies to bury.

Some people abandoned their sick loved ones.

Some doctors and priests refused to provide care.

The world was also in deep political and economic trouble. For Julian's entire lifetime, England waged the Hundred Years' War. Peasants rebelled against taxation and exploitation, and the social order of feudalism was falling apart.

Violence was a fact of life.

At the same time, authoritarian hierarchy and control was ramping up in the late medieval Roman Catholic Church, as the church clung to power in a changing world. This was a time of intense and carefully ordered social and churchly hierarchies.

People were terrified of dying of the plague without receiving last rites.

Rumblings of critique against the church—the kind of rumblings that would eventually become the Protestant Reformation—were afoot. Questions were asked about access to the Bible in English, about the authority of the church and of the pope, and about the role of the church in salvation.

And the church was cracking down on those rumblings by burning people as heretics.

There was intense anxiety about bodies. People knew contagion could be passed body to body, but it was not clear exactly how. Blood and guts and bodily fluids were threats to be contained.

Human bodies were feared as dangerous and polluting.

It seemed like the world was falling apart.[6]

And it seems like our world is falling apart.

We fear for our health and that of our loved ones.

We're tempted to put our own safety and security before that of others.

We're terrified of economic collapse.

Where we should be able to turn there for the gospel of grace, too many of us are hurt by sin in the church.

We may look for scapegoats and search for someone to blame for the pollution we fear (in the United States, acts of racism against Asians and immigrants come to mind).

We know fear. We know terror. We know sleepless nights.

Julian's world was crumbling, too.

---

6. Much of this reflection was informed and inspired by a wonderful book by Frederick Bauerschmidt, *Julian of Norwich and the Mystical Body Politic of Christ* (Notre Dame: University of Notre Dame Press, 1999).

THE BLOOD OF JESUS FOR A WORLD IN NEED

And yet.

She would turn us toward the cross of Christ.

She tells us to look steadily at Jesus. She reminds us that he is with us and for us. She asks to see the abundance of Christ's blood spilled for us.

Here is her account of one of her visions of Jesus's blood:

> Great drops of blood fell down . . . in the spreading out they were bright red. . . . The abundance was like the drops of water that fall off the eaves of a house after a great shower of rain, which fall so thick that no man can number them. . . . Because of their roundness, the drops were like the scales of herring as they spread over the forehead. . . . This showing was alive and active, and hideous and dreadful, and sweet and lovely. And of all the sights it was the most comfort to me that our God and Lord, who is so worthy of respect and so fearsome, is also so plain and gracious; and this filled me with delight and security of soul.[7]

She wants us to see that Jesus is real. That his blood and body are real. That he is here for us.

This is only one of many descriptions she gives of the blood of Jesus. Copious. Abundant. Flowing.

Julian is not ignoring the turmoil of the world. She's telling us where to look so that we can live in that world.

Where the plague destroys, the blood of Jesus flows.

Where some put their own safety over those who need them, Jesus draws near.

Where violence threatens, Jesus is our refuge.

Where human leaders would impose hierarchy, Julian saw the blood of Jesus flowing for all, making no distinctions between priest and sinner, rich and poor, healthy or sick.

Where the church creates false obstacles between us and God, Julian saw that the blood of Jesus clears those barriers away.

---

7. Julian, *Revelations of Divine Love*, 7.

And where people were scared of bodies and blood, Julian offered the grace of God.

Jesus's body, Jesus's blood, covers and heals.

The blood of Jesus is his intimacy with us. It's been poured out for us. It's flowing freely in a world that seems to be crumbling. He is with us. He is for us.

"For truly," says Julian, "it is the most joy that can be, as I see it, that He who is highest and mightiest, noblest and worthiest, is also lowliest and meekest, most friendly and most gracious."[8]

I'm praying today, with Mother Julian, to turn my eyes to the cross.

> For in him all the fullness of God was pleased to dwell, and through him God was pleased to reconcile to himself all things, whether on earth or in heaven, by making peace through the blood of his cross. (Col 1:19–20)

Holy God,

When it seems our world is crumbling, remind us that your goodness is sure. Where we ache, help us turn to you for solace. Be with all who are terrified. And remind us of Jesus and his care for us. Remind us that his blood is free for all.

In the name of the Father, the Son, and the Holy Spirit,

Amen.

---

8. Julian, *Revelations of Divine Love*, 7.

The Kind God Makes Us Kin

I'M QUARANTINED WITH MY kids. Many of my friends are quarantined with their kids.

It's hard.

Sure, it can be wonderful and precious, and all that. But it's hard.

Other friends are quarantined alone.

Also hard.

While I'm struggling with patience with the kids, I can also get a snuggle. Houses without snuggles are their own special kind of difficulty right now.

Some of us are separated from family in unusual ways. Cut off from hugs from loved ones. Unable to visit or receive visits in hospitals or nursing homes. Some of us are feeling the anxiety of heightened awareness about the vulnerability of family members.

This time is making us extra aware of all the feelings about family.

Every nerve ending is bare to the joys and the sorrows. The preciousness and the losses. The hurts and the unbelievable beauty. The great tenderness of everyday interactions and the great difficulty of living with others or living without others.

Family matters.

Julian of Norwich knew all this in her bones. Before she became an anchoress, she lived the household life. After her enclosure, and certainly after grief, she knew what it was to live alone.

And she drew on all of that in ways that help us to know God.

Julian wants us to know the kindness of God.

God is kind.

God is kin (the root of the word "kind").

God is family.

In Jesus, we are sons and daughters of the Father. In Jesus we are made kin to God and wrapped in the kindness of God.

Julian is famous for using images from home and family to describe God's love for us.

She describes Christ as our mother.

This image is surprising for many contemporary Christians, but it has deep roots in Christian history and fits with Scripture.[9]

It is Jesus, after all, through whom we are born again (John 3:5).

That's a mothering image.

And Jesus, lamenting over Jerusalem, cries, "How often have I desired to gather your children together as a hen gathers her brood under her wings" (Luke 13:34).

Jesus sees himself as our mother hen.

Julian reflects on mother love. She may be thinking of her own mother, or of children she bore and buried.

"The mother's serving is most near, most willing, and most certain."[10]

She knows that God's love for us is near, willing, and certain. As near, willing, and certain as Jesus himself.

---

9. If you want to know more about medieval mother imagery for Jesus, check out Caroline Walker Bynum's *Jesus as Mother: Studies in the Spirituality of the High Middle Ages* (Berkeley: University of California Press, 1984).

10. Julian, *Revelations of Divine Love*, 60.

In fact, she says, only Jesus can mother us in the truest, fullest sense:

> This fair lovely word "mother" is so sweet and so kind in itself, that it cannot truly be said of anyone nor to anyone except of Him and to Him who is true Mother of life and of all.[11]

Our families fail us. We fail our families. I'm excruciatingly aware of my failures as a mother this week, shut in the house with my brood of four.

Human mothers fail. Jesus our mother does not.

Human fathers fail. God our Father does not.

Julian brings in imagery from childbirth;

Jesus "carries us within Himself in love, and labors until full term so that He could suffer the sharpest throes and the hardest birth pains that ever were or ever shall be, and die at the last."[12]

And when things get hard, Jesus, like the best of mothers, "wills not that we flee away . . . but He wills then that we follow the behavior of a child, for when a child is distressed or afraid, it runs hastily to the mother for help with all its might."[13]

Whatever our human family situation is during this crisis,

whether it is too close or too far,

whether we face challenges of intimacy or challenges of loneliness,

or both,

Jesus is here for us.

He is nearer than a mother to her nursing child. Jesus is inviting us to run into his open arms.

---

11. Julian, *Revelations of Divine Love*, 60.
12. Julian, *Revelations of Divine Love*, 61.
13. Julian, *Revelations of Divine Love*, 61.

Heavenly Father,

Thank you for inviting us to become your sons and daughters. Thank you for your great kindness to us. Remind us of Jesus, who would gather us under his wings.

In the name of the Father, the Son, and the Holy Spirit.

Amen.

God's Response to Sin Is Jesus

THIS TIME OF DEEP fear and suffering brings with it claims that the virus is a punishment from God.

In times of great distress, people have always made such claims. Certainly, when the plague decimated medieval England, there were those who saw it as God's wrath. Groups of flagellants would even walk the streets, whipping themselves, trying to take on the punishment so the plague might pass.

But this is not the God who is revealed to us in Scripture.

Julian of Norwich understands what is wrong in calling a plague a divine punishment.

The key is Jesus and what he has done for us.

Julian was a young woman when she received the revelations, or "showings," she would later recount in writing. She was gravely ill, and everyone believed she would die.

There's a lot in those visions, but they focus most on Jesus and on the physical realities of his suffering and death on the cross. She saw him scourged, and "plenteously bleeding," and dying.[14]

In the depth of her illness, she tells us, she "wished to look up from the Cross," but she "dared not."[15]

---

14. Julian, *Revelations of Divine Love*, 12.
15. Julian, *Revelations of Divine Love*, 19.

PART II | PRAYING WITH JULIAN

Why would she not look away?

Because she knew "while I gazed on the Cross I was secure and safe."[16]

She had thoughts to look elsewhere. Perhaps she should look instead up to heaven. But God helped her know to keep her eyes on Jesus.

"So was I taught to choose Jesus for my heaven. . . . This has ever been a comfort to me."[17]

Jesus is the truth about God. The love of Jesus is the truth about God.

Jesus on the cross is the truth about God's love for us. Jesus on the cross tells us what we need to know about him—about Jesus himself—but it also tells us what we need to know about God the Father and God the Spirit.

For these three are one. And Jesus's love for us is the truth about God.

"God is love" (1 John 4:8).

The penalty of sin has been taken on by Jesus.

God is not exacting punishment through a virus.

The price of sin has been paid by Jesus. Full stop.

We don't need to take it on in self-flagellation or in looking for sinners to blame for our current suffering. Yes, the world still groans under the weight of sin, and everything wrong with the world—including this crisis—is part of that. But God's response to sin is Jesus.

God the Father is not some punishing horror. God the Father is the Father of Jesus, who died on the cross for love of us. The pain of this crisis is pain Jesus feels. He suffers with us and for us.

We can look at the cross and know that God is love.

---

16. Julian, *Revelations of Divine Love*, 19.
17. Julian, *Revelations of Divine Love*, 19.

GOD'S RESPONSE TO SIN IS JESUS

"For God so loved the world that he gave his only Son, so that everyone who believes in him may not perish but may have eternal life" (John 3:16).

Jesus is our heaven.

"See what love the Father has given us, that we should be called children of God; and that is what we are" (1 John 3:1).

We stand in the confidence of what Jesus has done for us.

> And we have seen and do testify that the Father has sent his Son as the Savior of the world. God abides in those who confess that Jesus is the Son of God, and they abide in God. So we have known and believe the love that God has for us. (1 John 4:14–16)

Julian wrote two accounts of her showings. The first, a shorter one, shortly after she recovered from her illness. The second, longer account was written many years later.

Julian spent those years dwelling on what God had shown her.

Keeping her eyes on the cross.

Fixing her eyes on Jesus.

Wanting to understand.

And finally, she got her answer:

"Wouldst thou know thy Lord's meaning in this thing?"

"Be well aware: Love was His meaning."

"Who showed it thee? Love."

"What showed He thee? Love."

"Why did He show it thee? For love."

Years of looking to Jesus taught Julian one thing.

"Love was our Lord's meaning. And I saw full certainly in this and in all the showings, that before God made us, He loved us, and this love was never slackened nor ever shall be."

"In this love He has done all His works, and in this love He has made all things beneficial to us, and in this love our life is everlasting."[18]

---

18. Julian, *Revelations of Divine Love*, 86.

O give thanks to the God of heaven,
> for his steadfast love endures forever. (Ps 136:26)

Dear God,

We need your love today. We need it so. We ask that you would bring us comfort in what you have done for us in the cross and in the resurrection. Remind us to look at Jesus and to know the truth of your love.

In the name of the Father, the Son, and the Holy Spirit,

Amen.

Hope Instead of Cheer

My social media feeds are full of memes and quotes admonishing me to look on the bright side. People are sharing prayers meant to remind me of my privilege, to remind me that it could be worse.

(I am the privileged person these posts are aimed at. My suffering, for the moment at least, *is* restricted to being quarantined. I'm not a health care worker or a grocery store clerk. I am not caring for a sick loved one. But each time I see a post like this, I remember that they are hitting lots and lots of people for whom it *is* worse. How must it feel to be the illustration of how bad things can be?)

And still for me, with my limited suffering, this thing is so hard. I wrote above about how it's okay to grieve because life is good, and precious, and beloved of God.

Should we remember those who are suffering most? Yes. Will there be silver linings? Yes. Can God work to bring good out of evil? Absolutely.

But this thing is bad.

And these posts are well meaning, but they ignore the weight of all we're bearing right now and the weight of what we still have to bear.

Mother Julian of Norwich struggled with this too. She wrestled with why God would allow sin, evil, and suffering.

And—in what are probably her most famous words—she received this from Jesus:

> Sin is inevitable,
> but all shall be well,
> and all shall be well,
> and all manner of thing
> shall be well.[19]

Julian isn't making light of sin and sorrow. She knew its weight and knew it well. Don't forget that she experienced the plague twice. She knew loss, and she knew grief.

And she doesn't have a narrow understanding of sin.

> In this unadorned word "sin," our Lord brought to mind generally all that is not good, and the shameful despising and the uttermost tribulation that He bore for us in this life, and His dying, and all the pains and sufferings of all His created things, spiritually and bodily . . . all pains that ever were or ever shall be.[20]

Knowing the full weight of sin and of sorrow, the Spirit enabled Julian to reach toward God and God's future in the confidence that "all shall be well."

Julian is asking us to lean forward into the space of heaven. Not to be chipper. Not to paste on a smile. Not to reprimand others for groaning under the weight of the crisis.

But to lean into and yearn for the fulfillment of the promises of God.

> Because of the tender love that our good Lord has . . . He comforts quickly and sweetly, meaning thus: "It is true that sin is the cause of all this pain,
> > but all shall be well,
> > and all shall be well,

---

19. Julian, *Revelations of Divine Love*, 27.
20. Julian, *Revelations of Divine Love*, 27.

HOPE INSTEAD OF CHEER

and all manner of thing shall be well."[21]

Paul is saying something similar in his words to the Corinthians:

> So we do not lose heart. Even though our outer nature is wasting away, our inner nature is being renewed day by day. For this slight momentary affliction is preparing us for an eternal weight of glory beyond all measure, because we look not at what can be seen but at what cannot be seen; for what can be seen is temporary, but what cannot be seen is eternal. (2 Cor 4:16–18)

Sin is weighty,
but the weight of glory?
It is everything.

I am praying today, not to deny the weight of suffering, but to put my trust in the God who has promised that, through it all, and finally, "all manner of thing shall be well."

Gracious God,

Thank you for the witness of your servant Julian of Norwich, who shows us how to lean toward you in faith and hope. Remind us of Jesus, who carried the weight of our sorrow and in whom we may find comfort and hope.

In the name of the Father, the Son, and the Holy Spirit, Amen.

---

21. Julian, *Revelations of Divine Love*, 27.

PART III

Psalms of Lament

God Hears Our Cries

IN THIS REFLECTION, I have only one thing I want to say:
God hears our cries of lament.

God is there, ready to receive our sorrows and pain.
Scripture gives us permission to lament.
Scripture tells the truth about the pain of the world, and we can bring that pain to God. God will hear our cries.

We can pray with the psalmist:

> O God, why do you cast us off forever?
>> Why does your anger smoke against the sheep of your pasture?
>
> Remember your congregation, which you acquired long ago,
>> which you redeemed to be the tribe of your heritage.
>> Remember Mount Zion, where you came to dwell.
>
> Direct your steps to the perpetual ruins;
>> the enemy has destroyed everything in the sanctuary.
>
> (Ps 74:1–3)

(Has God cast us off? No. Does God know that we may feel as though he has? Yes. Can we cry out with those feelings to God? Yes.)

PART III | PSALMS OF LAMENT

> We do not see our emblems;
>> there is no longer any prophet,
>> and there is no one among us who knows how long.
> How long, O God, is the foe to scoff?
>> Is the enemy to revile your name forever?
> Why do you hold back your hand;
>> why do you keep your hand in your bosom?
>
> (Ps 74:9–11)

(When we don't see how God is working, can we bring that to God in prayer? Yes. When we feel trapped, as though our sorrow does not end, we can call out to God).

> Remember this, O Lord, how the enemy scoffs,
>> and an impious people reviles your name.
> Do not deliver the soul of your dove to the wild animals;
>> do not forget the life of your poor forever. (Ps 74:18–19)

(When things seem hopeless, we can name it before the Lord our God.)

> Have regard for your covenant,
>> for the dark places of the land are full of the haunts of violence.
> Do not let the downtrodden be put to shame;
>> let the poor and needy praise your name.
> Rise up, O God, plead your cause;
>> remember how the impious scoff at you all day long.
> Do not forget the clamor of your foes,
>> the uproar of your adversaries that goes up continually.
>
> (Ps 74:20–23)

(This isn't pretty. No saccharine sweetness here. It's raw need. And God would have us bring it.)

Scripture gives us permission to lament.[1]

God hears our cries.

I'm praying today to remember to bring my sorrows and the sorrow of the world to the God who always hears.

---

[1] If you're interested in the biblical practice of lament, I highly recommend Soong Chan Rah's excellent book *Prophetic Lament: A Call for Justice in Troubled Times* (Downers Grove: InterVarsity, 2015).

Lord God,
    You hear our cries. Please hear them now, and remind us of Jesus, who is with us in our sorrow.
    In the name of the Father, the Son, and the Holy Spirit,
    Amen.

On Not Being Okay

A few days ago, I was worried about my son. The boy is hard to read. And I asked my husband if he thought our son was okay.

My husband said, "Honey, none of us are okay right now."

And I relaxed a little bit at the truth of his words. Right now is hard.

We're facing enormous uncertainty. We expect what comes next to be rough.

For me, this comes with anxiety and fear, and . . .

I'm not okay.

I can see that someone might look at me and think, "Well, she seems to be fine. She's writing devotions."

But I'm not fine. These devotions are a little cry against the pain around me. A little hope that I might be able to share courage with others in reminders that Jesus is with us in our pain. Sometimes, I find a little courage here myself.

But I'm not okay.

(You can hear how I'm using "okay" as an understatement, right? A stand in for words that are too hard to say.)

But Scripture gives us words.

ON NOT BEING OKAY

Scripture does not shy away from the truth about all that is not okay.

Take one of the many, many psalms of lament, Psalm 88:

> O Lord, God of my salvation,
>   when, at night, I cry out in your presence,
> let my prayer come before you;
>   incline your ear to my cry.
>
> For my soul is full of troubles,
>   and my life draws near to Sheol.
> I am counted among those who go down to the Pit;
>   I am like those who have no help,
> like those forsaken among the dead,
>   like the slain that lie in the grave . . .
>   My eye grows dim through sorrow.
> Every day I call on you, O Lord;
>   I spread out my hands to you . . .
>
> But I, O Lord, cry out to you;
>   in the morning my prayer comes before you.
> O Lord, why do you cast me off?
>   Why do you hide your face from me?
> (Ps 88:1–5, 9–10, 13–14)

Today I am praying to take all my not-okay-ness and, in it, to cry out to the Lord.

Holy God,
  Hear our cries. And remind us of Jesus, who entered into the hurt of this sinful world and joined us in crying.
  In the name of the Father, the Son, and the Holy Spirit,
  Amen.

Lament for Injustice

IN SCRIPTURE, THE PRACTICE of lament is not only lament for individual sorrow. Lament is also lament for the community, lament for others who are suffering, and lament over the injustice of this sinful world.

We lament injustice, because God is the God of justice.

So much injustice is on my heart and in my prayers as we begin to understand the consequences of this pandemic. This plague is heightening economic and racial injustice. It makes the vulnerable more vulnerable, and it preys on those who are already in need. Asian Americans are experiencing racist attacks. In Chicago, black people are dying from the disease at almost six times the rate of white people.

The words of Scripture help us to see and name this injustice and teach us to call out to our just God:

> Rise up, O Lord; O God, lift up your hand;
>   do not forget the oppressed.
> Why do the wicked renounce God,
>   and say in their hearts, "You will not call us to account"?
>
> But you do see! Indeed, you note trouble and grief,
>   that you may take it into your hands;

LAMENT FOR INJUSTICE

> the helpless commit themselves to you;
>   you have been the helper of the orphan.
>
> Break the arm of the wicked and evildoers;
>   seek out their wickedness until you find none.
> The Lord is king forever and ever;
>   the nations shall perish from his land.
>
> O Lord, you will hear the desire of the meek;
>   you will strengthen their heart, you will incline your ear
> to do justice for the orphan and the oppressed,
>   so that those from earth may strike terror no more.
> (Ps 10:12–18)

Today, I am praying in lament for the ways the injustice of this world is being heightened in this time. I am praying that God's people may learn to see injustice and work for God's righteousness for all.

Dear God,

    We know that you see, that you note trouble and grief, that you take it into your hands. Help us to be like you in this, and remind us of Jesus, who welcomes all who are vulnerable and hurting to come to him.

    In the name of the Father, the Son, and the Holy Spirit,
Amen.

Telling the Truth

I think Christians sometimes shy away from the practice of lament because we think we'll sound whiny or ungrateful.

But lament is a deeply biblical practice. It is a holy and healthy practice because it is a practice of truth-telling.

When we cry out to God, naming our pain and the pain of the world, we are telling the truth about life in this world of sin.

We are truth-tellers because God *is* the truth.

We are truth-tellers because Jesus is "the way, and the truth, and the life" (John 14:16).

We are truth-tellers because the Spirit of truth dwells in us (John 15:26).

And so we can and do lament.

Lament gets at one of the biggest truths of all: the truth that the groaning and pain and devastation of the world are not the way things are supposed to be.

They are signs of a world gone wrong, signs of a world where the effects of sin range far and wide.

When we call them out as such, we are telling the truth about the God who sees what is broken and promises to heal. We are telling the truth about our need.

The psalmist cries out, naming pain and brokenness. At the same time, behind and beyond that pain and brokenness, the psalmist rests on the steadfast love of God. Lament speaks the truth about hurt. And lament speaks the truth about the God who is with us in our pain.

This pattern—naming pain while also pointing to the God who heals—is typical of many of the psalms of lament. Take Psalm 13:

> To the leader. A Psalm of David.
>
> How long, O Lord? Will you forget me forever?
> > How long will you hide your face from me?
> How long must I bear pain in my soul,
> > and have sorrow in my heart all day long?
> How long shall my enemy be exalted over me?"
>
> Consider and answer me, O Lord my God!
> > Give light to my eyes, or I will sleep the sleep of death,
> and my enemy will say, "I have prevailed";
> > my foes will rejoice because I am shaken.
>
> But I trusted in your steadfast love;
> > my heart shall rejoice in your salvation.
> I will sing to the Lord,
> > because he has dealt bountifully with me.

As children of the God who is truth, we can tell the truth about all that is broken. I'm praying today to seek God's truth in all my words and prayers.

Holy God,
   You are the way, the truth, and the life. Help us to see and speak the truth about pain and suffering, and remind us of Jesus, who came to be truth and to bring truth to heal all that is broken.
   In the name of the Father, the Son, and the Holy Spirit,
   Amen.

Love and Lament

TODAY, I HAD PLANNED to be on a once-in-a-lifetime spring break trip with my family. Today, I get to tell my kids that we're postponing another planned vacation.

Today, there are more than a million cases of the disease worldwide, more than a quarter million in my own United States.

Today, I'm beginning to hear of diagnoses and deaths from the virus touching people I love: Someone in a loved one's church. Someone else's grandparent. Someone in a community I adore.

Today, I'm trying to settle into a season that will bring more and more losses and in which I still need to live and work and love.

Today, I am excruciatingly aware of the finitude and frailty of human plans and human life. And somewhere, deep beneath and beyond and through and with that, I am aware that we're being held up and held together by the unchanging and steadfast love of God.

And today I lament. And, today, I pray with words from Psalm 90:

> A Prayer of Moses, the man of God.
>
> Lord, you have been our dwelling place
>   in all generations.

Before the mountains were brought forth,
> or ever you had formed the earth and the world,
> from everlasting to everlasting you are God.

You turn us back to dust,
and say, "Turn back, you mortals."
> For a thousand years in your sight
> are like yesterday when it is past,
> or like a watch in the night.

You sweep them away; they are like a dream,
> like grass that is renewed in the morning;
in the morning it flourishes and is renewed;
> in the evening it fades and withers.

For we are consumed by your anger;
> by your wrath we are overwhelmed.
You have set our iniquities before you,
> our secret sins in the light of your countenance.

For all our days pass away under your wrath;
> our years come to an end like a sigh.
The days of our life are seventy years,
> or perhaps eighty, if we are strong;
even then their span is only toil and trouble;
> they are soon gone, and we fly away.

Who considers the power of your anger?
> Your wrath is as great as the fear that is due to you.
So teach us to count our days
> that we may gain a wise heart.

Turn, O Lord! How long?
> Have compassion on your servants!
Satisfy us in the morning with your steadfast love,
> so that we may rejoice and be glad all our days.
Make us glad for as many days as you have afflicted us,
> and for as many years as we have seen evil.

PART III | PSALMS OF LAMENT

Let your work be manifest to your servants,
    and your glorious power to their children.
Let the favor of the Lord our God be upon us,
    and prosper for us the work of our hands—
    O prosper the work of our hands!

Holy God,

    Though our flesh is like grass, your steadfast love is forever. Thank you for binding us in your love as we lament. And turn us to Jesus, who took on our flesh for the sake of love.

    In the name of the Father, the Son, and the Holy Spirit,
    Amen.

PART IV

The Way of the Cross

Pour It Out

(Written for the Beginning of Holy Week 2020)

Jesus knows the week ahead is fraught with danger.
   He is preparing to pour himself out for us.
   What do you do when what's coming is the brutality of the cross? If you're Jesus, you have dinner with your friends.

We probably know the cast of characters—Lazarus, Mary, and Martha.
   The two sisters and their brother are some of Jesus's closest friends. He calls them "beloved." He comes to their home when he needs respite.
   The last time he was here, he stood at his friend's grave.
   And he wept.
   And then he called Lazarus forth from the dead.
   And now the friends are having a meal together, again.
   Even if we don't know this story, the one of the dinner party we're at right now, we might be able to predict what they're doing tonight based on the other stories we've heard about them.
   Martha is serving. She's made sure the meal will be good. She's looking out to see that everyone has what they need. Maybe she pauses to glance at her brother, marveling that he's living and breathing, after she thought she'd lost him forever.

Lazarus is at the table with Jesus. They're dipping bread in oil and eating fish. Maybe Lazarus is conscious of enjoying the food and the company more than he would have before he got sick and died.

Before his friend Jesus called him out from death and back to their shared table.

Do they talk about it? The fact that that the Lord of Life is at their table?

And what of the other sister? Where is Mary tonight?

She's where she's been before. At the feet of Jesus.

She takes a jar of "costly perfume made of pure nard" (John 12:3).

She anoints Jesus's feet.

She wipes those feet with her hair.

Tears run down her face.

She knows what Jesus is about to say out loud. She knows she will not always have him there, with her. And she prepares him for his death by pouring all she has out for him, a preview of what he will do for her when he goes to the cross.

The house fills up with the "fragrance of the perfume."

It's Monday of holy week.

The way of the cross lies before Jesus.

It lies before his friend, Mary.

It lies before us, too.

Several years ago, I was thinking about Mary and her alabaster jar of perfume. About how costly it was. I was doubting I'd have it in me to do what she did.

But then I thought about some other jars in Scripture: clay jars.

"We have this treasure in clay jars," Paul says, "so that it may be made clear that this extraordinary power belongs to God and does not come from us" (2 Cor 7:7).

I wrote this short poem:

never, Lord, would I have had the guts
to shatter that alabaster jar.

Love, though, made me clay.

whatever nard
   still spilling
   through the
   cracks,

so graciously set free.

It's holy week, and the way of the cross is before us. It will probably be the strangest Easter of our lives.

All the alabaster things are shattering.

We're left with clay that cracks, clay that makes it clear that our hope is in God and God alone.

After the bit about the clay jars, Paul goes on:

> We are afflicted in every way, but not crushed; perplexed, but not driven to despair; persecuted, but not forsaken; struck down, but not destroyed; always carrying in the body the death of Jesus, so that the life of Jesus may also be made visible in our bodies. For while we live, we are always being given up to death for Jesus' sake, so that the life of Jesus may be made visible in our mortal flesh. (2 Cor 4:8–11)

Our mortal flesh is groaning. The cross looms before us.

And it's right here, in our weakness and sorrow, that grace will make Jesus "visible in our bodies."

I'm praying today, to look to the cross, to focus on what Jesus did in pouring himself out for us, so that God's grace might allow me, just a little, to make Jesus more visible right here.

PART IV | THE WAY OF THE CROSS

Dear God,

Thank you for your promise that, though we are afflicted, we will not be crushed. Help us to look to Jesus, who poured himself out on the cross, and so made it possible that we might show his life to the world.

In the name of the Father, the Son, and the Holy Spirit,
Amen.

Jesus Shares Our Grief

Jesus is on the path that leads to the cross.
    We are on the path that leads to the cross.
    People want to see him. I don't know what they're expecting.
    Probably something glorious.
    We want to see him?
    What are we expecting?

And Jesus says, "The hour has come for the Son of Man to be glorified" (John 12:23).
    There we go. Bring on the glorious.
    Bring on the triumphant king and the defeat of oppressive powers.
    Bring on the parades and the choirs of angels.
    Bring on the cake and the champagne.
    But that's not the kind of glory Jesus has in mind.

"Very truly, I tell you, unless a grain of wheat falls into the earth and dies, it remains just a single grain; but if it dies, it bears much fruit" (John 12:24).
    Gulp. Is Jesus talking to us? Are we the grains of wheat, falling into the earth to die?

PART IV | THE WAY OF THE CROSS

Where's the shiny glory we want?

Jesus's glory is the glory of the cross. Jesus's glory is the glory of the grain of wheat, buried in the earth. Jesus's glory is the glory of his life poured out for love.

"Whoever serves me must follow me, and where I am, there will my servant be also. Whoever serves me, the Father will honor" (John 12:26).

Jesus calls us into the hidden glory of the cross. He calls us into the hidden glory of following him. He calls us into the shadowed places. And he is with us there.

He is with us here.

"Now," he says, "my soul is troubled. And what should I say—'Father, save me from this hour'? No, it is for this reason that I have come to this hour" (John 12:27).

Jesus came for the hour when cathedrals would be turned into hospitals. Jesus came for the day when New York City would have to bury the dead in mass graves. Jesus came to share my grief, your grief, our grief.

Jesus is with us in the depths of our suffering. He goes with us to the grave. He is with us in this holy week of dread and terror. Though we don't see it, his hidden glory embraces and surrounds us, binding us in his love.

Lord God,

You have shown us that you are nearer to us than our own breath, especially in our time of terror. Remind us of Jesus and his glory, even here and now. Especially here and now.

In the name of the Father, the Son, and the Holy Spirit,

Amen.

God with Us

Jesus knows the cross is coming.
We know the cross is coming.
Jesus "was troubled in spirit" (John 13:21).
I am too.

Jesus had plenty of reason to be troubled. He was at a meal with his disciples, his friends, and after he identified Judas as the one who would betray him, Judas left the table to give Jesus up to the authorities.

Betrayal would lead to suffering, would lead to death. A chain of events was set in motion that would culminate in nails being driven through Jesus's body.

Trouble indeed.

We, too, have plenty of reason to be troubled.

And Jesus is with us.

Jesus "was troubled in spirit." This—right here—is the central mystery and the central good news of the Christian faith. It is the truth that Jesus, who is God, has truly become one of us and shares in all that is ours, including the hardest things and the most grievous days.

PART IV | THE WAY OF THE CROSS

Jesus shares every crisis with us.

Jesus shares this pandemic with us.

This is the truth of the incarnation.

Maybe you've known this truth for years. Maybe you've never heard of it before. In both cases, it is good news. Right here. Right now.

The word "incarnation" means "in the flesh."

Jesus is God. When he comes to us, born of Mary, he is God in the flesh. He is God with hands and feet. He is God who will be troubled. He is God with us and for us.

The book of Hebrews celebrates the deep comfort in this truth:

> Since, then, we have a great high priest who has passed through the heavens, Jesus, the Son of God, let us hold fast to our confession. For we do not have a high priest who is unable to sympathize with our weaknesses, but we have one who in every respect has been tested as we are, yet without sin. Let us therefore approach the throne of grace with boldness, so that we may receive mercy and find grace to help in time of need. (Heb 4:14–16)

Jesus is with us in our weakness. Jesus shares our humanity "in every respect."

Jesus is the Lord of the Universe,
the king of kings,
the eternal Son of the Father,
the most high.

This very Jesus enters our frailty, our sorrow, our finite flesh.

He didn't just act like one of us. He *became* one of us. He *is* one of us.

And we are attached to him and, at his side, we stand before the throne of grace.

Jesus is with us and for us. Jesus knows our troubled spirits. He knows our aching hearts. He knows grief and loss. He knows our physical pain. He knows what it is to walk by faith through the valley of the shadow.

His troubled spirit is the truth of God's love for us.

Today, I am praying to bring my troubled spirit to Jesus and to know that he is with me.

Holy Father,

In your great love, you have sent to us your only son, Jesus Christ. As we face the cross, remind us of Jesus's troubled spirit. Remind us that we are not alone.

In the name of the Father, the Son, and the Holy Spirit,
Amen.

Love to the End

(From Maundy Thursday)

It's the hardest week of Jesus's life.

Tomorrow brings the cross.

"Jesus knew that his hour had come to depart from this world and go to the Father. Having loved his own who were in the world, he loved them to the end" (John 13:1).

Jesus's last move? Loving us to the end.

> Jesus, lover of my soul,
> Let me to Thy bosom fly,
> While the nearer waters roll,
> While the tempest still is high:
> Hide me, O my Savior, hide,
> Till the storm of life is past;
> Safe into the haven guide;
> O receive my soul at last.
> —Charles Wesley

Jesus loves us through pain, suffering, sorrow, and death. He ends his life with love.

LOVE TO THE END

Jesus, knowing that the Father had given all things into his hands, and that he had come from God and was going to God, got up from the table, took off his outer robe, and tied a towel around himself. (John 13:3-4)

He belongs to the Father. He is the truth about God.
Jesus, our savior and our God, ties a towel around himself.
Jesus, the Lord of creation, pours water into a basin.
Jesus, who was and is and is to come, kneels to wash the feet of his friends, uses the towel to dry their feet.
Jesus takes the lowest task and does it for love.

Other refuge have I none,
Hangs my helpless soul on Thee;
Leave, oh, leave me not alone,
Still support and comfort me.
All my trust on Thee is stayed,
All my help from Thee I bring;
Cover my defenseless head
With the shadow of Thy wing.
—Charles Wesley

Jesus is the truth about God. God is Love. No task is beneath Love's notice. No pain is outside Love's reach. No person is denied Love's care. Jesus covers us in love.

He reaches for us, even when some of us aren't having it.

"You will never wash my feet," says Peter.

"Unless I wash you," Jesus replies, "you have no share with me" (John 13:8).

All the feet washed, including Peter's, Jesus returns to the table. "Do you know what I have done to you?" (John 13:12).

I think they, like us, have only the barest inkling of what Jesus has done. They know something of his majesty and beauty. They rightly call him "Teacher and Lord," but it's impossible for them or for us to see how great the mercy is, that the Lord of the Universe should kneel at our feet.

We can't understand, but we can praise.

> Thou, O Christ, art all I want;
> More than all in Thee I find;
> Raise the fallen, cheer the faint,
> Heal the sick and lead the blind.
> Just and holy is Thy name,
> I am all unrighteousness;
> Vile and full of sin I am,
> Thou art full of truth and grace.
> —Charles Wesley

Jesus leads them, leads us, to follow his example, to do as he has done:

"If I, your Lord and Teacher, have washed your feet, you also ought to wash one another's feet" (John 13:14).

> Plenteous grace with Thee is found,
> Grace to cover all my sin;
> Let the healing streams abound;
> Make and keep me pure within.
> Thou of life the fountain art,
> Freely let me take of Thee;
> Spring Thou up within my heart,
> Rise to all eternity.
> —Charles Wesley

Jesus loves us sinners and transforms us. He has covered our sin and made us new. He makes it possible for us to love to the end.

> I give you a new commandment, that you love one another. Just as I have loved you, you also should love one another. By this everyone will know that you are my disciples, if you have love for one another. (John 13:34b–35)

Today, I am praying to lean in to Jesus, who is Love. And, in this hard holy week, I am praying that his Spirit might enable me to love as he has done.

Lord God,

You have shown us the depths of your love in Jesus kneeling at the feet of his friends. As we face the cross, help us to do so with Jesus, held in his love.

In the name of the Father, the Son, and the Holy Spirit, Amen.

Jesus against the Enemy

(From Good Friday)

Today we need to talk about death.

And there is lots of talk of death, in this time of plague and fear.

Some argue that efforts to prevent the spread of the virus are less than Christian. These people claim that Christians should not fear, or even—it seems—try to avoid death.

Some heap scorn on mitigation efforts, arguing that such efforts betray an undue love of this life, a materialism, a worldliness inappropriate to the Christian whose hope is in eternity.

Some argue that the old and the weak are fair game for the plague, that the deaths of these who were "on their last legs" are a small price to pay.

Good Friday reveals this for what it is: bad theology. It is bad theology because it ignores God hanging on the cross.

It fails to fix eyes on Jesus, carrying the cross to the hill where nails will pierce his flesh.

"So they took Jesus; and carrying the cross by himself, he went out to what is called The Place of the Skull, which in Hebrew is called Golgotha" (John 19:16–17).

Anyone who would make light of grief or mortal danger forgets that Jesus took on the horror of death itself—and it was and is a horror.

Jesus endured the pain of death in order to destroy death.

God doesn't destroy something if it doesn't need destroying. Death is an enemy.

(To be sure, death is a conquered enemy, but today, we don't get to go there. Today, we look on Jesus, dying on the cross.)

"There they crucified him, and with him two others, one on either side, with Jesus between them" (John 19:18).

Good Friday reveals death for what it is. Death is a horror. Death is the consequence of sin. Death had Jesus weeping at his friend's grave, and death ravaged Jesus on the cross.

"'It is finished.' Then he bowed his head and gave up his spirit" (John 19:30b).

How can we look on Jesus on the cross and suggest that any death is a small price to pay?

Does a small matter merit the blood and water flowing from Jesus's side, opened for us?

"One of the soldiers pierced his side with a spear, and at once blood and water came out" (John 19:34).

Jesus died because he loves human life and wants us to love the life we have in him. Jesus died for this world, not so that we could discount this world.

The Christian faith isn't about eternity against the world. It's about the world being taken up into eternity.

The fourth-century church father Athanasius wrote about the weight of Jesus's death on the cross.

He reminds us that "all" of us "were due to die," but Jesus offered his "sacrifice on behalf of all, surrendering His own temple to death in place of all, to settle [our] account with death and free [us] from the primal transgression."[1]

Athanasius pictures Jesus on the cross, his arms "outstretched" to embrace us all.

---

1. Athanasius, *On the Incarnation*, 4. I've been teaching Athanasius's *On the Incarnation*, ed. and trans. John Behr (Crestwood, NY: St. Vladimir's Seminary Press, 2014) for more than fifteen years, and it is always a student favorite.

Here, he says, a "marvelous and mighty paradox ... occurred, for the death which they thought to inflict on Him as dishonor and disgrace has become the glorious monument to death's defeat."

Not a monument to death's smallness.

Not an encouragement to embrace death.

A monument to death's defeat.

In Jesus, a mighty enemy has fallen. Let's not call the enemy anything but what it is.

> They took the body of Jesus and wrapped it with the spices in linen cloths, according to the burial custom of the Jews. Now there was a garden in the place where he was crucified, and in the garden there was a new tomb in which no one had ever been laid. And so, because it was the Jewish day of Preparation, and the tomb was nearby, they laid Jesus there. (John 19:40–42)

The Lord of Life was placed in the tomb. His body was cold. His heart and breath were stilled. Nothing could be more terrible. Nothing could make it more clear that we are right to fight against death, and to grieve when it comes, even as we await Jesus's full and final victory over it.

Today I am praying to keep my eyes on the cross as I live with death, to look and

> See from His head, His hands, His feet
> Sorrow and love flow mingled down
> Did e'er such love and sorrow meet
> Or thorns compose so rich a crown?
> —Isaac Watts

Lord God,

Today we remember the death of our savior, Jesus Christ our Lord, who revealed death for what it is and in whom death was destroyed. Help us to look to Jesus and know your love for us and for every human life.

In the name of the Father, the Son, and the Holy Spirit, Amen.

PART V

Resurrection

Weird Easter

SHELTERING IN PLACE, QUARANTINING against coronavirus, many of us experienced the most unusual Easter of our lives.

Yesterday, my family celebrated what my husband kept calling "weird Easter."

It was discombobulating. It was not what we wanted.

But it was a celebration nonetheless.

Quarantine can't stop Easter.

Usually, we put on spring finery.

Yesterday, we wore pajamas. (My youngest might have worn the same Spiderman pajamas he'd had on for a week.)

Even in our pajamas,

> Christ the Lord is risen today, Alleluia!
> Earth and heaven in chorus say, Alleluia!
> Raise your joys and triumphs high, Alleluia!
> Sing, ye heavens, and earth reply, Alleluia!
> —Charles Wesley

It's weird Easter, but it's still Easter.

PART V | RESURRECTION

Usually, we hurry to get to church early, because we know the sanctuary will be overflowing with people.

Yesterday, we slept in.

Even with sleep in our eyes,

> Love's redeeming work is done, Alleluia!
> Fought the fight, the battle won, Alleluia!
> Death in vain forbids him rise, Alleluia!
> Christ has opened paradise, Alleluia!

It's weird Easter, but it's still Easter.

Usually, my church reverberates with majestic music, choral procession, the organ playing with drums and strings and brass, voices to the sky.

Yesterday, we watched church on the TV screen, and my husband and I sang, while our kids stared or mouthed the words.

Even with teenagers who won't sing,

> Lives again our glorious King, Alleluia!
> Where, O death, is now thy sting? Alleluia!
> Once he died our souls to save, Alleluia!
> Where's thy victory, boasting grave? Alleluia!

It's weird Easter, but it's still Easter.

Usually, church is followed by a joyful frenzy of an egg hunt.

Yesterday, we had quiet Easter baskets at home.

Even when we're not feeling it,

> Hail the Lord of earth and heaven, Alleluia!
> Praise to thee by both be given, Alleluia!
> Thee we greet triumphant now, Alleluia!
> Hail the Resurrection, thou, Alleluia!

It's weird Easter, but it's still Easter.

Usually, we have tons of friends over to the house for an Easter potluck feast.

Yesterday, only our immediate family sat down at the table for the ham, cheese potatoes, and cake.

Even as we're unable to be together with the community we love,

> King of glory, soul of bliss, Alleluia!
> Everlasting life is this, Alleluia!
> Thee to know, thy power to prove, Alleluia!
> Thus to sing, and thus to love, Alleluia!

It's weird Easter, but it's still Easter.

Usually, we rejoice because the Lord of Life has conquered the grave, even though our lives are still full of grief and hard things.

Yesterday, we rejoiced because the Lord of Life has conquered the grave, even though our lives are still full of grief and hard things.

Today, I am praying to rejoice because the Lord of Life has conquered the grave, even though life is full of grief and hard things. Today, the joy of Easter is reality, even while the strange pain of this time is reality too.

Death and isolation and grief do not stop the truth of Easter.

The grave could not hold him. Death was defeated. Christ is risen indeed.

Dear God,

Thank you for the joy of Easter, even in the midst of pain. Remind us of Jesus, the risen Lord, who triumphed over sin and death.

In the name of the Father, the Son, and the Holy Spirit,

Amen.

Easter between the Times

THESE QUARANTINED DAYS, I'M feeling hope ebb and flow a thousand times a day. There's plenty of hopelessness, plenty of discouragement.

What can I do with that, when I know that the Christian life is a life lived by faith, a life lived in hope?

I have to live with the fact that, while God's work in our lives is very, very real, we don't get to see that work in its fullness.

Yet.

We live in anticipation of something that is not yet in sight.

Jesus is risen from the dead.

But death still lives among us.

Theologians call this the "already/not-yet" of Christian life.

In Jesus, the kingdom of God has already come among us.

But that kingdom is not yet visible in its fullness and power, and we still groan under the tyranny and sin of the kingdoms of this world.

Already, Jesus is Lord of the universe, and God has "highly exalted him," giving "him the name that is above every name" (Phil 2:9).

EASTER BETWEEN THE TIMES

Not yet is it the case that "at the name of Jesus every knee should bend, in heaven and on earth and under the earth, and every tongue should confess that Jesus Christ is Lord to the glory of God the Father" (Phil 2:10–11).

Already Jesus has defeated the grave.

Not yet has that day come when those who have died will be raised like him.

Already our King has come: born, lived, died, and risen from the dead.

Not yet has our King returned, to "wipe every tear" from our eyes and fulfill the promise that

> death will be no more;
> mourning and crying and pain will be no more. (Rev 21:4)

And so, we live between the times.

Between joy and sorrow.

Between the first Easter and the last day, when "the dead in Christ will rise" (1 Thess 4:16).

Between the pain of dwelling with the ongoing power of sin and death in this world and the confidence that the Spirit is empowering us to fight against those powers.

Usually, Easter is a time of a lot of "already." It's joy and celebration and resurrection glory.

This weird Easter, we are more aware of the "not yet." We groan and grieve even as we look to Jesus in hope.

We know that hope comes with doubt.

And we can and do grieve, but not "as others do who have no hope" (1 Thess 4:13).

The already of Jesus is the pledge that the not yet will become the already.

"For since we believe that Jesus died and rose again, even so, through Jesus, God will bring with him those who have died" (1 Thess 4:14).

PART V | RESURRECTION

In Easter, between the times, we grieve. But we also look forward in hope.

Paul hopes that we will "encourage one another with these words" (1 Thess 4:18).

Between the times, encouragement is not about bright words and saccharine sentiment.

En-couragement is to instill courage.

Encouragement is to offer hope that has a basis in reality.

Courage has its basis in Easter, even and especially between the already and the not yet.

Today, I'm praying to find courage in the only place where courage truly is: in the resurrection of Jesus.

Loving God,

Thank you that you are the basis of our hope, even when we cannot see it. Remind us of Jesus, whose resurrection in the already is our hope for the not yet.

In the name of the Father, the Son, and the Holy Spirit,

Amen.

Labor Pains

It's the Wednesday morning after Resurrection Sunday.

We've barely begun the Easter season, but I'm not feeling the resurrection joy.

Instead, the "not yet" of this weird Easter is hammering at my brain, as I think about professional and family realities and anxieties and uncertainties in this time of pandemic.

When will we know what's next?
Not yet.
When will I see my parents again?
Not yet.
When will my kids go back to school?
Not yet.
When will I hug a friend?
Not yet.
The not yet and the not knowing is corrosive.

My painful not yets don't even name the deep theological not yet, the not yet-ness of that last day when God will finish the work of making all things new.

Still, my personal, painful not yets are part of that deepest theological reality.

PART V | RESURRECTION

They're a part of the pain of "the body ... dead because of sin" (Rom 8:10), of the "sufferings of this present time" (Rom 8:18), of creation itself being "in bondage to decay" (Rom 8:21) and "groaning in labor pains" (Rom 8:22).

Most human beings, in most times and in most places, have lived with pain and uncertainty that resembles our pandemic reality far more than it looks like what we think of as normal.

Most human beings, in most times and most places, have been aware that death looms near.

The most unusual thing about life in the twenty-first century may be that wealth and technology have insulated many of us from acknowledging the nearness of death.

But death has always been near.

We've always been finite and fragile.

And we've always had to keep living and loving and doing the work of loving God and loving neighbor. We've had to do that right in the midst of our finitude and fragility.

I love that Paul uses the metaphor of labor pains to talk about the groaning of creation and of human beings as we walk through the not-yet.

As a mother, it's a metaphor I can feel in my bones.

And it's a metaphor that gives me a glimpse of the joy that lies on the other side of this pain. My flesh memory of the pain of labor and the joy of holding my newborns helps me dwell in this not yet, because of the promise that

> if the Spirit of him who raised Jesus from the dead dwells in you, he who raised Christ from the dead will give life to your mortal bodies also through his Spirit that dwells in you. (Rom 8:11)

LABOR PAINS

First Easter is the pledge of everlasting Easter. Jesus's resurrection promises our own. That doesn't make the not yet any less painful. But it might help us to keep living and loving through it.

Paul endures the not yet as he looks toward a future of final resurrection. All creation groans, and we join in:

> And not only the creation, but we ourselves, who have the first fruits of the Spirit, groan inwardly while we wait for adoption, the redemption of our bodies.
> (Rom 8:23)

And we're not alone in this groaning. The Spirit "helps us in our weakness" (Rom 8:26).

And we are given the strength to keep moving, to keep living, to keep loving.

> What then are we to say about these things? If God is for us, who is against us? He who did not withhold his own Son, but gave him up for all of us, will he not with him also give us everything else? . . . Who will separate us from the love of Christ? Will hardship, or distress, or persecution, or famine, or nakedness, or peril, or sword? . . . No, in all these things we are more than conquerors through him who loved us. For I am convinced that neither death, nor life, nor angels, nor rulers, nor things present, nor things to come, nor powers, nor height, nor depth, nor anything else in all creation, will be able to separate us from the love of God in Christ Jesus our Lord. (Rom 8:31–32, 35, 37–39)

Today, I am groaning. But I am also praying to remember that I am groaning inside the world where the Spirit has already raised Christ from the dead.

I am groaning in the world where the Spirit promises to help as we wait for full and final victory.

I am groaning in a world where there is pain, but where that pain cannot separate us from the love God.

PART V | RESURRECTION

Lord God,
    We give you praise for your promise to be with us in the groaning. We give you praise for your promise to deliver us into new creation. Remind us of Jesus, whose love for us is known in his death and resurrection.
    In the name of the Father, the Son, and the Holy Spirit,
    Amen.

Continuity and Transformation

THOUGH DEATH WALKS AMONG us, resurrection gives us strength for the journey.

Though this journey seems interminable, God promises a future of hope and healing.

Though it seems impossible to keep going, the risen Christ and the power of his Holy Spirit are with us, offering us resurrection power.

Christian teaching about resurrection has two parts:

1. the resurrection of Jesus, and
2. the resurrection of the rest of us.

In 1 Corinthians 15, Paul connects the resurrection of Jesus to the resurrection of all the dead. In fact, he connects them so intimately that we can't have one without the other. Because Christ has been raised, so will those who have died also be raised.

> Now if Christ is proclaimed as raised from the dead, how can some of you say there is no resurrection of the dead? If there is no resurrection of the dead, then Christ has not been raised; and if Christ has not been raised, then our proclamation has been in vain and your faith has been in

vain.... If for this life only we have hoped in Christ, we are of all people most to be pitied. (1 Cor 15:12–14, 19)

Jesus's resurrection results in our resurrection.

Jesus's resurrection is "the first fruits of those who have died" (1 Cor 15:20).

In faith, we expect our own resurrection to follow the pattern of Jesus's. It's a pattern of continuity and transformation.

Resurrected Jesus is continuous with Good Friday Jesus. The tomb is empty. He carries the scars of crucifixion. He is still friends with his friends, and he still does his Father's work. He's the same Jesus.

But resurrected Jesus is also transformed. He does a lot of appearing and disappearing, sometimes people recognize him, but sometimes they don't, and he has been set free from death.

This pattern of continuity and transformation is good news.

It's good news that Jesus is the same Jesus. We need him. Not someone else.

And it's good news that Jesus, in his resurrected flesh, has defeated death. In this time of pandemic, where death looms near, we long for that transformation.

Paul tells us that our resurrection—the resurrection of those who die in Christ—will follow the pattern of Jesus's; "Just as we have borne the image of the man of dust, we will also bear the image of the man of heaven" (1 Cor 15:49).

We look in faith toward resurrection transformation in our lives, in our own souls and bodies.

From perishable to imperishable.

From dishonor to glory.

From weakness to power.

From selfishness to being led by the Holy Spirit.

All that transformation is the best of news, as God promises to set us free from sin and death and works with us to transform us into the image of Jesus. We need it.

CONTINUITY AND TRANSFORMATION

But continuity is also good news.

The body now and the resurrection body are both body.

They're stuff, they're flesh, they're continuous with the persons we are in the here and now.

As Jesus was the same Jesus after his resurrection—eating with his friends and bearing his scars—we will be the same people we are now, when God finishes the good work of transforming us into new creation.

We are embodied souls, and in God's future, we will still be embodied souls. This means that we matter to God. Our hands and feet matter. Our flesh and thighs matter. Our lives matter. The lives of all who are precious to us are precious to God as well.

Paul sings out the good news:

> When this perishable body puts on imperishability, and this mortal body puts on immortality, then the saying that is written will be fulfilled: "Death has been swallowed up in victory." "Where, O death, is your victory? Where, O death, is your sting?" (1 Cor 15:54–55)

Having pointed us to the future, Paul turns us back to the present.

The future matters for the here and now.

Because of resurrection,

> Be steadfast, immovable, always excelling in the work of the Lord, because you know that in the Lord your labor is not in vain. (1 Cor 15:58)

Because God will transform all that is broken in us and in our world, bringing healing and victory over sin and death,

> Be steadfast, immovable, always excelling in the work of the Lord, because you know that in the Lord your labor is not in vain. (1 Cor 15:58)

Because God will bring us—body and soul—into new creation,

PART V | RESURRECTION

> Be steadfast, immovable, always excelling in the work of the Lord, because you know that in the Lord your labor is not in vain. (1 Cor 15:58)

Because Christ has been raised, and we will follow where he has led,

> Be steadfast, immovable, always excelling in the work of the Lord, because you know that in the Lord your labor is not in vain. (1 Cor 15:58)

Today I am praying that the Spirit might pour the power and strength of the resurrection over the people of God, so that we might find the courage and steadfastness to continue in God's work, knowing that our "labor is not in vain."

Dear God,

You are the God of resurrection. You are the God who loves the world enough to work to make it new. Help us to love as you would have us love, and remind us of Jesus, whose resurrection victory over sin and death is our power to persevere in a world where death seems to reign.

In the name of the Father, the Son, and the Holy Spirit,

Amen.

In My Side

THOUGH JESUS IS RISEN from the dead, Thomas has not seen him.

Though Jesus is risen from the dead, Thomas does not yet believe.

But then his Lord appears before him in the flesh and greets him: "Peace be with you."

Jesus shows Thomas the marks of crucifixion still visible on his hands.

Then, Jesus invites Thomas to "reach out your hand and put in my side" (John 20:27).

Thomas knows Jesus by his wounds. Thomas acknowledges Jesus, crying out, "My Lord and my God" (John 20:28).

The Italian artist Caravaggio depicted this scene in his famous painting *The Incredulity of Saint Thomas*. The painting emphasizes the physicality of Jesus's resurrection. There are no halos glowing there. The figures are portrayed in natural, even rugged, style.

Jesus guides Thomas's hand into the gaping hole in his side.

When it was painted at the beginning of the seventeenth century, Caravaggio's painting evoked controversy. Some found its realism unsettling. Surely it was too physical. Some wanted idealism in their religious art, not yawning wounds.

But the stark materialism of Caravaggio's work coheres with a key theological point. It fits with the doctrine of the incarnation and the truth of Christ as God made flesh. It fits with the bodily nature of the resurrection.

And it fits with the way God chooses to meet our needs. We, who are groaning, body and soul, are invited to come in to the body of Christ, to come near to Jesus himself, to be united with him, body and soul, and to be comforted, body and soul.

Brutal materialism is good Christology.

It fits with the truth that the resurrected Jesus is with us and for us.

In this time of pandemic, two of my children seem to need extra snuggling. They don't use words to describe what living through this is doing to them, but I know their need. I know it because they keep coming to my side, pressing against me, leaning their heads into my body.

It's no wonder that we need comfort, body and soul, for that is the way God made us, and it is where God meets us.

We're invited to come to Jesus's side.

As we continue to face uncertainty,
Jesus invites us to his side.
As we suffer grief and loss,
Jesus would have us find comfort in him.
As we feel the magnitude of hurt and pain,
Jesus waits for us with open arms and open side.
Jesus would draw us to his very body.
Would have us,
"Reach out your hand and put in my side" (John 20:27).

Some have seen Jesus's next words to Thomas as a rebuke, but they can better be read as a warm promise. Jesus promises to bring us in, even as he has invited Thomas in.

He is still here for us, body and soul.

"Have you believed because you have seen me? Blessed are those who have not seen and yet have come to believe" (John 29:20).

Along with the rest of the signs recorded in his Gospel, John tells us that his account of the risen Lord has been "written so that you may come to believe that Jesus is the Messiah, the Son of God, and that through believing you may have life in his name" (John 20:38).

In his side, we can find abundance in the midst of scarcity,
comfort in the midst of fear,
and life in the midst of death.

I'm praying today that we may know that his body is open for us and that he tenderly invites us to come in.

Lord God,

We give you praise as the one who did not withhold your only Son but sent him into the world to take on all that is groaning under the weight of sin, including the pandemic and all it brings. Remind us of Jesus's wounded side and his desire that we might be joined to him.

In the name of the Father, the Son, and the Holy Spirit,
Amen.

Keeping On

I wrote these reflections daily over the first five weeks my state was on stay-at-home orders.

Since then, Illinois has seen four more weeks of lockdown, and we expect at least two more.

Despite my useless efforts to control the situation by sifting through the news, constantly refreshing the numbers, and searching for evidence that the curve charting the virus's path might be flattening, it remains the case that there is so much we don't know.

As I write these closing words for *Pandemic Prayers*, we don't know true numbers for infections or mortality rates. We don't know how to treat the virus effectively. We don't know when the church will gather again in person. We don't know what will happen in the United States as some states open up and others stay locked down, and we don't know if school will open in the fall or what things will look like if it does. (This last one is especially anxiety provoking for my mother's and teacher's heart . . .)

Though life with the novel coronavirus has been declared the "new normal," it doesn't feel normal, and it hurts.

Fear remains.
Uncertainty remains.
Finitude remains.

How do we keep on going?

How do we do the work we need to do to love God and love our neighbors in a situation we can't control?

One answer to this question is this:

We do it day by day.

And we can do it day by day because God is with us.

When God's people wandered in the wilderness, the food God provided was food for each day.

Bread came down from heaven, not once, but again and again and again. Manna was there for each new day, and when people tried to save it for the future, it became worm-ridden rot.

When Jesus taught us to pray, he encouraged us to ask our Father for "daily bread." Christians have often heard this petition as a reference to the daily nature of the manna God provided for Israel.

We don't know the future, but we know the character of God, who gives good gifts to us, his sons and daughters.

Though we can't see the future, God is faithful.

Though we can't control outcomes, God is love.

Though tomorrow may bring new suffering, God will be here with us and for us through it all.

We are finite. We are not God. We cannot know or control the future, but God promises that we will find grace for each new day.

When I talk to my college-age students about human finitude, I try to help them think about it as a gift. We may rant against our limits, but in the gift of finitude, we receive something that fits our humanness. Finitude reminds us of the good news that God is God, and we are not. Finitude teaches us daily reliance on God.

And then we have to learn it again.

And again.

Each. New. Day.

And in the gift of finitude, the Spirit empowers us to pay attention to the daily work before us. We're called to do the work of each new day.

PART V | RESURRECTION

We're called to love, right here and now.
God is who God is.
God is love.

And, as the prophet spoke it, the "steadfast love of the Lord never ceases, his mercies never come to an end; they are new every morning; great is your faithfulness. 'The Lord is my portion,' says my soul, 'therefore I will hope in him'" (Lam 3:22–24).

I am praying today, for you, dear reader, and for myself, that we might turn to the Lord anew each morning, seeking the grace to love through each day.

Dear God,

Thank you for your steadfast love. Thank you for the mercies you pour upon us, new every morning. Through fear and uncertainty, we pray that we would remember that you are with us. Thank you for being the God who provides daily bread. In suffering, remind us of Jesus, who shares our grief and who let us know your faithfulness.

In the name of the Father, the Son, and the Holy Spirit,
Amen.

Afterword

BETH FELKER JONES'S BOOK of prayers and reflections has been a gift. Like many during the coronavirus pandemic, I have found myself searching for resources. Indeed, early in the pandemic, I went back and reread Albert Camus's *The Plague*, for example, and tried to find information on the church during other pandemics. I kept searching for books on the history of viruses and the ways other countries addressed public health crises in the past. All in an attempt to keep up. It was exhausting.

Then, as a follower of Beth on Facebook, and as a fellow colleague, I began to notice how she was posting prayers and other pieces about the pandemic. I saw how she was drawing on a wide array of sources, both theological and spiritual. She was reflecting deeply on what was taking place during this troubling time and seeking to understand the life of faith in light of God's love. Here was someone, I thought, who was providing nourishment for those who were sheltering in place and finding ways of dealing with faith and family, church and culture, in the face of the COVID-19 outbreak. I found in Beth someone who had sought a way to bring together the riches of Scripture and tradition on the one hand and the experience of our situation on the other, all to communicate hope. I wondered how we might expose Beth's work to a wider audience, not just online but through print. This book is the result.

AFTERWORD

As a pastor during this season, I have also tried to stay current on the latest postings and resources on how to maintain health and well-being. Like many, I have been versed as of late in the practices of social distancing and in the lessons of reopening a local congregation to worship in person. I have had to learn how to go online and stream services and discover new ways of staying connected. The pandemic has brought to the surface new challenges to the practice of ministry and new stress points as well. Dealing with the unknown is never easy. In addition, there were the old and persistent questions of theology itself: Where is God amidst the suffering? How do we comprehend evil in light of Christ's life, death, and resurrection? Where do we seek and find hope? Thankfully, Beth offers reflections on these questions in a way that persons can discuss and contemplate, either privately in devotion or corporately in a small group. Her invitation to us is to explore doctrines like the Trinity, incarnation, resurrection, cross, and discipleship within a framework of generosity, if not encouragement. What she offers is nothing less than a demonstration of what John Wesley called "practical divinity"—pointing us toward love of God and neighbor and growing in faith. The insights she brings from persons like Julian of Norwich and Martin Luther (both of whom also lived through plagues of different sorts) reminded me of how this pandemic is not the first time the church has had to contend with sickness on a grand scale.

I offered to write this short afterword as a way to show gratitude for this book of prayers. I hope to share it with the people I serve. In a day when we are looking for light in darkness and for hope amidst despair, this little book is a gift. Read it and be fed, pray it and receive God's grace!

ANDREW D. KINSEY
Season of Easter
Franklin, Indiana

Andrew D. Kinsey is the senior pastor of Grace United Methodist Church in Franklin, Indiana. He also serves as one of the editors to the Wipf and Stock series on Wesleyan Doctrine and as editor to *Notes from a Wayward Son: A Miscellany* and *The Logic of Evangelism Revisited*, also by Wipf and Stock.

About the Author

BETH FELKER JONES TEACHES and writes theology at Wheaton College in Wheaton, Illinois, where she lives with her husband, children, and dogs. She holds the PhD in theology from Duke University and is the author of books including *Practicing Christian Doctrine: An Introduction to Thinking and Living Theologically* and *Faithful: A Theology of Sex*.

Find her on Twitter @bethfelkerjones

Made in the USA
Columbia, SC
08 April 2021